The
Truth
Squad

The Truth Squad

DENNIS SCHMITZ

 Copper
Canyon
Press

Printed in the United States of America.

Cover art: Bosch, Hieronymus (1450c.–1516), *Estrazione della pietra della follia* (*The Extraction of the Stone of Folly*). Copyright Scala/Art Resource, NY, Museo del Prado, Madrid, Spain.

Copper Canyon Press is in residence under the auspices of the Centrum Foundation at Fort Worden State Park in Port Townsend, Washington. Centrum sponsors artist residencies, education workshops for Washington State students and teachers, Blues, Jazz, and Fiddle Tunes Festivals, classical music performances, and the Port Townsend Writers' Conference.

LIBRARY OF CONGRESS
CATALOGING-IN-PUBLICATION DATA

Schmitz, Dennis, 1937–
The truth squad / Dennis Schmitz.
p. cm.
ISBN 1-55659-182-9 (pbk. : alk. paper)
I. Title.
PS3569.C517 T78 2002
811'.54—DC21
2002002761

9 8 7 6 5 4 3 2 FIRST PRINTING

COPPER CANYON PRESS
Post Office Box 271
Port Townsend, Washington 98368
www.coppercanyonpress.org

To Alex,
Rosali,
Victoria,
Josephine,
&
Sophia

ACKNOWLEDGMENTS

Some of these poems have appeared in
the following publications, and grateful
acknowledgment is made to their editors:

Alaska Quarterly Review
The Best of Crazyhorse
Caliban
Crazyhorse
Dog Music
Field
The Geography of Home
Harvard Review
Hayden's Ferry Review
Hubbub
The Journal
Pacific Review
Plum
Quarterly West
Raccoon
South Florida Poetry Review
What Will Suffice

Contents

Part
One

The Truth Squad

Roped against the bridge pier so that
his tired legs can scissor down

more compressor hose, Chicago's last
sandblaster kicks from one graffitied

meaning to another, his free hand kneading
over his face a rubbery other face

& glassed eyeholes as the compressor
overhead accelerates into rapturous bursts.

It's the same sexual noise he sucks
through the gritty mouthpiece, panting

as he works. Gang tags, laments & manifestoes
crackle away under his pistol's hissed-out

spellings. I read what he denies
from the next bridge over. Behind me

all Dearborn Street is stalled, paraphrasing
where its cars want to go. My own car's

sideways across both lanes, your plea squawking
on the cell phone. I've flipped

open the trunk for spray cans;
two cars back, another commando is beginning

to letter a Honda's windshield.
Determined others rappel down the Wrigley

Building's white sides.
At least one of us will write your secret.

Rumpelstiltskin

Straw into gold—what's technology's
dwarf-name that our princess sent

out so many courtiers to recover?
The anthropologists brought back Ishi,

who took a whole day
to manipulate tule roots into a simple basket,

the too-short discards loose
against one lab wall... & the same dwarf

inside my laid-off neighbor told him to divide
his Volvo into six jobs he must do

before the aerospace industry could prosper.
The dwarf must've lost the servodrive—

for a whole June the loose parts,
entrails of the Volvo's electric windowlifts,

one gizmo of lubricant-shiny gears
& glossy plastic like a tiara

glittered in his yard's yellowing grass.
If the neighbors I won't name hadn't kept

the baby they shouldn't have tried to make,
I'd name the clinic that would've churned

it into ectoplasm by the title of this poem.
My neighbor's face got redder

behind the wedged-shut glass
each time he drove the wife through

false labor. "Ishi" is ironic—
why did the whites name him "man"

in a language he didn't know,
all of his tribe posthumous in the poor basket

he'd made, "the last California
wild Indian"—the last speaker of his own

language, the curses of which he must've mumbled
into the cot mattress. Above him in the lab night

bows, arrows, & many, many baskets he'd tried
for the tribe's sake to make true...

& who'll ever know—what if he had been Klutz,
the tribe's worst weaver,

now dwarfed by what he had to do?
Whose riddle, whose child, whose gold?

Deficit

The boy's pencil corners the eight-point buck
in the snow he couldn't make

out of anything but deficit—
blank paper into which

a low, leafless bush fuzzes because
earlier the buck, gut-ripped, writhed

over it into this foreground
flawed with wolves. Once out

of the pencil his buck thrashes
to return, stepping its own entrails

into the snow. One wolf's so black
from the furious pencil

that the boy, worried,
wipes where the black won't wipe

away as it spreads up his finger-ends.
His mother summons the boy part of him

unsuccessfully to family
meal, but he's in the deficit,

arguing his own appetite—
first the pencil, then his paw prints

blackening the page.

Dumpster Diving

The Safeway checker's lost count
at me & lets the whole line
know he's the fundamentalist God—

halfway back to Jesus,
a woman complains, *Hurry up
& pay* as I'm begging to pay

for the bum behind me
who's palpating a cheap six-pack & shuffling,
as we all shuffled this far

in the store's version of retributive
justice, edibles bagged with taxables
& lottery tear-offs each sweats to deserve.

I insist, I whine in my own kind of Muzak.
I get louder, *He's society's scapegoat!*
My fingers grab at the man's rags

as he bobs up from the floor.
He's with me, I say, because I had witnessed
him squirm out of the rainpants &

plastic coat wired shut at the wrists.
He'd been Dumpster diving in the store's alley
for two-cent empties (stamped flat),

the redeemables, for a store chit
which he now shows like a stigmata in one palm
as the six-pack pulls him higher,

& I resolutely try to hang on,
his dirty shoes in the candy bars,
then his head nudging the ceiling neon.

No doubt syphilitic & peppered
with lice—how little he owes any of us.

Dances

        Right on stage
pulling, wrestling each
        other by shirtfront, manic,
the two puppeteers
ad-lib anger for the matinee

friends or relatives who came unprepared
        for human drama,
the smaller cardboard puppet stage
kicked flat,
shirt buttons scuffed into squeals

underfoot—neither wants to be the puppet
        Godiva, neither wants
to be the hand,
all Stanislavsky, inside her.

      ·◆·

        At once cleaning
himself with paper
        towels, his mind on call-waiting
or maybe directed
by radio signals, the retired cop's still law

to the storefront
where the legal poor are fed
            castoffs, where they chew
in synchronized groups like lab assistants

            forced to eat test failures.
He's in blues
with insignia snipped off
            but sure he's not one of them—
like the woman he just wrestled

back to her alley,
            her child around
his leg, wading with them
to a dance tune the child can't stop

            screaming, all three briefly
in step, sliding
over polyurethane trays slimed shiny
            with beef grease & noodle loops,
he jigsawing one arm

            over her arm,
the loose earplug of his pocket
radio making a welt on her face.

Paradise

for Raymond Roseliep

Man dozes while God designs sleep,
the eighth day of creation.
Angels' wings lick the commercial

weather of Paradise—
even the fib, bucktoothed,
is beautiful. But only enough sleep

is left over to make a single
corpse—so it is we enter heaven
one by one. Though lovers

would sleepwalk
each other's bodies, our dreams
can repeat only the duplicity

of the senses. The poet's work
is to whittle blue
sky out of the high forks of the florid

maple, to make night from one
owl & with his own night sweat to wash
enough talk to wake each of us

the other side of sleep.

Because the Eye Is a Flower Whose Root
Is the Hand,

the zoo raccoon lifts its food pellet,
& out of Genesis

the Flemish tapestry Eve shows
the apple is an object

instinct truculently makes Art.
Look & look on your knees in the small

yard as you work
the fallen earring (its coral

a tapestry knot)
from the knotted clover. Each green

clinging in the clover dozens
is a claim for Art, is a way for the earring

to survive as praise
for a way of looking.

Wanting Definition

Mongrel need & the fire
distributed equally: one dog

& two men (shirt-sleeved)
in the Chicago cold, Osso's asphalt

lot. Osso's garbage drum kicked
over, righted & lit

might be a man—
his heat too flakes off rust,

he gasps at his own little fire,
the urine smell.

Osso's barman, last shift,
walks a grating across

the street window, 2 AM.
The accordioned fittings

squeal. He leans there
in shirtsleeves for the woman

customer who takes up
her sleeping man's drink, nudges

him & curses out loud his tiny bohunk sex—
breath soaks the rest,

soaks even the metals where man
comes together: left-hand-

threaded bolts, socket wrench broken
off in a cloth-covered part,

navel zippers which close
with the sound of a voice

wanting definition,
wanting, if not fortunate singularity,

coupled torpor.

Frontier

Mold weeps through
the SP depot mural,
weeps through the wagons & the pioneers

more red-faced from the high fanlight sun
toward which a trapped
real bird beats, screaming

one accurate note against the depot noise,
its wings blurring
with the effort of staying

outside the picture.
Ignoring bird and mural both,
a sweaty woman with a baby

urges a boy to pull
harder at the stuck men's room door
which squeals as it opens

a rectangular cut of painted prairie
grass: a remodeler's joke
one kneeling pioneer seems to examine

as he plucks painted wheat heads
or a fugitive strawflower,
solitary in the crossed stems.

He won't show the flower to the others,
the artist seems to say, as he too keeps focus
on the mural's archaic purity,

the wide women,
the mix of men & draft animals—
equals in an Eden where Art leaves them.

Grossier's "The Passenger Pigeons"

is only painted-over cloth
muffling the steps of the painted hunters—

three nineteenth century men,
almost saintly in the corona sparking

off the guns of two.
Overhead, flocks are so dense

that a stored-up blackness stains
the hunters' upturned faces

as they pause between killing
& the responsibility of eating their prey

into extinction.
The dead mold to rocks in the clasping

foregrass, a violent Kansas,
maybe Oz my finger enters as I outline

what the card below calls "threatened
species"—what the killers can't kill

hides, the way it would in a child's
contour puzzle, the painter's solipsism:

the pointed ears of a kind of fox
are twisted into one rifle's mechanism,

a prairie dog is in two
trampled pigeons—the card says rare

reptiles tangle snout-to-snout
in a gesture the oldest hunter makes

to his friends.

Yosemite: 40th Anniversary Climb

Marriage too is a climb that
earlier couples teach us to go up

tandem, the upgrade partner
not pulling, as Vernal Falls thunders

both names. Forty years on foot,
but we're only an hour into this zigzag,

sweaty & cross. The last 300 feet up
are the splash, roil & glottal stops

of the Merced going down,
precipitous, some acre-feet per

minute, but only a blue thread to lost birds
wise to follow it through the granite

breakoffs & postglacial rock spill.
The air is mountain-cold, so our sweat dries

maps of labor or apprehension as it did
in Chicago forty years before

when we tried on vows two sizes big,
rethinking love. To the left, Illilouette

Falls is wispy on a far wall
2000 feet high where trees

are so small that they seem twisted
wires in the toilet's ventilating window

sawn eye-high; here I put on a symbolic
cardboard top hat—the foolish

uniform of one conscripted to love,
the hat's necessary elastic the same ellipse

my grin makes as I hand you the veil
I'd folded in my backpack. You won't pin

the veil in your hair because too soon
we're at a difficult synchronized pairing,

spidered out, exhausted above the Merced,
where we straddle spray, chain webbing wound

in our fists as we lean into the speech-hole
of the canyon—a momentum so dangerous

that the self is only an epilogue,
a downstream noise

in the rapids & useless to aver.
Love is first self-jeopardy

on a trail wide enough for only one,
but we totter up & wade

a vestigial side trickle the main stream outgrew
before it could throw itself whole

down the 300 feet we toiled up.
Dizzied, we stand on the granite lip—

behind us is the quarter-mile granite shelf
smoothed away since the Ice Age

by how many different drops of Merced water?
& above this falls, twice as high, is Nevada Falls—

which might be our task the next forty years.
Here I spill our picnic—Brie, bread knife,

the assertive long baguette I dub
"Freudian" & champagne crusted in foil.

Part
Two

•◆•

The Alien Corn

Kneeling to see the world
through the front door's mail slot & breathing

Iowa air so palpable it's chewy,
I pretend I'm bolted

into an alloy helmet
that won't leak the stories I had misspelled

deliberately so teacher couldn't leave
her math world for mine.

There's no way back, I whisper —
there is only the wreckage.

(I push the mail-flap wide to look out.)
Iowa will be twenty years long,

but I'll anecdote it into a paradise.
I'll have children with the natives —

Thy people shall be my people.
Twenty years for other spacecraft to punch

down in the soybeans. *Help,* I whisper.
Behind the barn, the farmer's daughter is beating

weevils from a cornskin rug. *Help! Help!*

Iowa Gothic

I

The men putting on bird costumes are in
the curtained part of the gallery.

The noise is the noise
of intent, the *rat-tat* of knives

on the zinc serving
counter, the *shh* of sawing dense meat;

the smells too are oriented
serially to the event.

Only the bride is tangential,
smiles as her mother puzzles a knot

out of the girl's hair.
What comes next is the multiplication

of desire: the heavy couples
dancing the accordionist into sweaty dissonance,

the disgraced collie & the lab
pounding gravy-stained noses & paws

against the building's one window,
whining to be let back in.

II

County fair or tent-healing,
I am the same despair

crawling the throat of any species—
the one they call to make

the mayor's hydrocephalic son dream
"land" for the last judging,

where the lame learn to envy
the snakes they handle

& as punishment everyone receives
what he or she asks for.

Always the tent fills out with groans
praising the One-Who-Is-Eaten.

My voice never wilts in the grand
champion's mouth as the judges

draw close: one to grip the moist
nose ring, another to heft

hidden parts or quote the buyer's
clues, the breeder's self-concern.

But when I am prayed
down into a perennial soured

by second-places, I must imitate meat
wincing in the fry-pan.

The Text

A five-day
rain, & our flooded 95-year-old cellar's
clay exfoliates
clods faster than the cellar pump,

autodidact, can catch the way
this story changed—
the pump's too-literal thirst

is to pucker dry the dirt walls;
its method is to thread hose into the dark

second meanings, its hose's kin,
the yard's elm roots, already know
as they surrender to text,

to the interrupting small rocks,
changing course & changing course to come
out in this cellar version of root heaven

& wash phosphorescent in currents
that the pump stirs.
I listen like one already wet

to the raining against what's man-made,
against roofs, the *ping* off windows—
but I catch only the talk of a bad listener,

not the conversation of equals.

Plums

Damn the birds (we didn't
see them, but wake

to their evidence) who,
myopic, pierced each fruit—

but never the same plum twice.
Those plums we can rescue,

oozing from the stem end
& vaguely sexual,

decay quickly. Cereal bowls,
even cups, whatever we could have

eaten from, brim with them.
Puckered skin—the weight of each

on each presses
out a kind of mucous

nourishment that later smells.
In our credulous torpor we did not eat.

Damn it! We did not eat.

Crabgrass

Poison or blowtorch
it—only a trace root

under the concrete, it will thread up,
the tiny sword leaves frill
into the walkway. *You scuff those leaves*

off, my mother, 78, jokes—*I'm too old*
(she's in tongueless garden shoes)

to dance.
What else can I do but take her
knotty hand, & we're lockarmed near
hibiscus & the field

roses she's knelt to clear of weeds,
stepping out
together. *God's misspellings,* she calls
the barely visible

focus of our inhibited polka, three
green crawlers, only crabgrass epithets,
three ur-flowers of the garden

walk, but survivors. *This is how I want to die,*
she gasps, her one arthritic foot

up, the other down in this design
            the crabgrass persists

in making.
            Pain is my unforgiving
partner, she says—*let me catch my breath.*

Farney's Sister

The storm expected for many days had tasted
of carbolic: lightning
pulled from tree to tree,
violent but short rains Farney's sister thought

she conjured over the straying
squash rows, over pole beans
supine but knuckling beanless onto their strings.
Such is the seniority of memory over desire

that, though my senses callus over,
fifty years after, I still smell the blackened
sweet potatoes ooze over our stick fire

under the WPA culvert.
In this picture the culvert cuts
off the popple-choked fields from the lawn & garden
over which Farney's sister sings

as she stamps the culvert roof,
whisking a gauze bag of lightning bugs
in parabolas at the end
of my dad's trout rod, her dress rucked

almost to the waist.
From fifty years away I see my little head look
out of the culvert arch.

The fire my two friends prompt
with throwaway boards or paper grows
as smoke pushes, swelling my clothes

with composite field smells.
But in this picture, I can't twist my head
(even now, here, as I remember which muscles)
to look up at Farney's sister, I can't.

Brothers

We never fought
        wars, though each
of us was the other's enemy
in models WW II taught us

        to cut side by side,
balsa ME-109 or the peerless Spitfire.
I was intent
though clumsy, younger, but my brother—
        how much he wanted

        the truth,
the in-scale blued cylinders, all flaps
& ailerons working
        off cockpit controls—
whatever it took to imagine flight

        or death from it.
Once he wanted blood—
not the pilot's coughed-back dying,
        not bravura spots,
but proof again
        of the will to fly on.
He reached out

the razor blade saying, *I'm afraid
to hurt myself,*
& after a pause,
his finger in the cockpit, *Cut me,*
he said, *cut me.*

Hands

The one-handed county agent, forgiven (as they said
then) military service,
though it was the forties & the enemy

only islands away, instead made what war
the county, pitying him,
ignored. Bored with early bed, I'd listen

for his truck's gearbox in spiel
& counterspiel argue
with the man's one-handed inattention,

closer by one more neighbor's pasture
to the tree stump my father,
relenting, had surrendered to the man's need

to kill the rest of him
with the county's faulty prewar dynamite
that might sizzle or just smoke

a limited incandescence.
Under me the urgent radio vibrated
the floorboards between

the adults & me, where I lay over
the war news, losing
piece by piece the hot bedroom as sleep

steadily counted off the dead,
adding even the hand our agent was owed
& all prostheses, down to the one-job cocked

chrome hooks that must've been bundled
in dozens, lefts singlemindedly with lefts—
or of themselves, they had crawled patriotically

across the guessed world
to finish soldiers, turn our boys avid again
for the hands of others.

Guadalcanal, Okinawa, Iwo Jima—
island by island we mistakenly forgave
every sin the war committed.

Maybe my father's later story to us lied
more about war than walnut trees
when he excused the stump as a tree he'd sold

for rifle stocks to a Wisconsin mill—
because we'd grown up pacifist to Wisconsin,
even when across the Mississippi

its farms annexed clouds we wanted,
& though my brother once saw
their distant farmers wave sickles

or hands (it was too far to tell) at us
while the west wind wrote
anger in the intervening poplars.

Klauer's Dog

The early sun all mane
but toothless on the frosted rooftops,
dirty news sack banging
at the knees, I'd go out to give Iowa
the sleepless Nazis

& the local sin it wanted more.
Who else would've carried the world
to Sienkiewicz, maimed out of 1943's

stateside Army (second floor,
rear)? NO. 28 had a deer knife pounded
handle-deep in the door, but the point facing
you had a tennis ball
over it, & NO. 40, it was gossiped,

had French-kissed the former newsboy.
My genius was to forgive everything.
I was George Brent in a Bette Davis weeper,
overacting under the weight

of truths so tawdry that I never grew.
Newsboy genetics made me
scrawny & so burdened with my own vision
that I had to hunch through

empathy's primitive two-step.
But today I forgive even Klauer's dog,

his shit so potent
the grass died into self-poisoning.
Short-leashed to his own temper,
he'd bite at anything that rippled
the weedy yard—over him all birds flicked

higher. Walter Mitty of the suicides,
I'd squeal the gate three times first;
I'd concentrate myself
so short that my human odor squeezed away,
so short that the absent Klauers

had to tack my pay doorknob-high.
On their porch I once saw four
sets of muddied kids' shoes
that had been walked to the shut door.

A poor family but the dog got fatter—
did the kids I never saw grow
move out, or did the dog eat them?
& then Klauer's dog too was gone, his chain

dogless but by habit taut in the long grass.
That winter I was taken
by what he had guarded, back past
ratty cardboard nailed over old doorways,

plumbing ends studding the house outer walls overhead,
cellulose insulation curling
like brown body hair from the clapboard
I touched until I could cross

into snow, at first gritty as Alka-Selzer,
then drifts, then universal white I waded
through, my empty news sack shadowing me
into a kind of path, trampled
kid-sized to the sumac grove I expected,

the short trees all prongs,
leafless & incestuously wrapping knobbed limbs
over one another. The refrigerator,
its short legs buried, the cylindrical

condenser on top like a robot's head,
had its door cracked
so that all of the Midwest winter

could flow out of it & into a kid's nightmare.
I was so short that I had to loop the news sack strap
to close the door until I breathed in

each of the other kids in there before me,
praying, praying to grow big & never die.

Part
Three

•◆•

The Three-Legged Dog

which I wanted as allegory
pushes its snout, all hair-commas & snot,

against my pants-leg.
The party's host coaxes in dog-patois, coaxes

both of us back from revulsion,
from Art. Up close, I see the actual

harness steadying some leg
device, studs & a leather-wound wood piece—

the dog wobbles
but moves. Neither of us is enticed

by sauce-painted
shrimps or the party canapés, but by despair,

a state so low man goes in
on all fours, either as dog

which prefers flesh,
or the ingenuous lamb which eats

its own mood.
The dog holds up its snout, & I look

into the loose-lipped cleft
at teeth, phlegmatic, the only one of its retinue

attentive.

Abbott's Lagoon

The storm's still everywhere I run,
affectionate like a lover who touches you

with pliers, at the periphery
of the ego, little wavelets like blisters.

The lagoon's surface is folded
in labial wind stirrings; a few birds twitch

in & out of the water onto the sand
that's the color of a rain-blasted trench coat.

Then, at the edge of the ocean,
I study three minutes (I time myself

to know when to wade in) the loose
mound in the backwash that's flexing

& bobbing in the ocean's insomnia.
Is it the suicide you always promise in the storm

against yourself, or just more kelp
torqued around its own embrace, loving

any sort of afterlife, self-tangled like all
of us, oozing the bottom's root-grease

into the water around it? Glad to be puzzled,
I step back, turn from all the evidence

& trot into another morning's workout.

Egoist

Sun's thrift: light & reflected
light interknit
an illusion on which the jeep birds

feed. The first two peck almost
       all the flashes
off the windshield, but a third, egoist, screams

because the engine's still on
of what he thinks is the world,
       & maybe he's frightened
at the way everything throbs
       with increments—

the hot jeep hood his claws can't grab onto,
the Pacific at a low tide grumble,
the screams of the bigger birds
       which the ranger scares

off the seal carcass (a runt, its wounds
licked fuzzy by water), rounded,
       abraded all over, its blackness sucking
back all light.
       Though *wanting* also means *insufficient,*
how the birds must want light

from the beach's bright things—
the beer can pulls, the translucent fire
of cellophane. How the birds hop

not to be dragged back into the black
egg, as cursing, the ranger loops
out steel cable
                from the jeep's winch to the carcass.

Carmel

Vulgar paw prints on the BMW
trivialize the threat, but the car's siren,

still in pique, pursues
a tired raccoon. A few valleys east,

California recites lightning over Sierra
foothills to curse the cheap

tract houses, but here animals still argue
the wilderness these raked white beaches

& millionaire "cottages" pretend.
Robinson Jeffers built rage first

then poems from the fog-scuffed rocks he bore,
grunting up from this same beach

to make a tower he could be tall in.
We stoop to enter Jeffers' world;

his wife would rap the low ceiling between them
until his pacing overhead stopped because

the poem might've squeezed in the whole
Big Sur coast. Miles south

& a real wilderness away, Hearst bought
an illusion too big for him—the shiploads

of statuary parodied in *Citizen Kane*,
the private zoo—only the red TOURIST arrow knows

its way through his castle's cluttered acres.
In Carmel, Loretta & I go out the gate

Jeffers used—now designer homes crowd it.
The BMW is local, the raccoon bred

to add to the car's relevance.
Prosperity is only a small god,

but you pray to it—just in case.

Base Metal

Troth might be spit passed
between two sets
of lips in the first teen kiss,

& probably infectious, but divorce,
Molly told us as she pre-empted the talk
of all around us & cut
her boudin with Loretta's borrowed

knife, divorce is the smell
under the recently removed ring,
not sweat itself, not the gold either,

sweating to stay on base metal.
She said you spent the first year of marriage
waiting for your finger to turn green

& the rest of it as a gold-enameled
Virgin, the beech paneling it's on, wormy.
Molly's hand had to relearn,

as mine did after the broken
wrist, attitudes of take
& release, accepting steadily-heavier goods,

as out of the cast it became human.
Molly's teen son had been passed

over a bridge of hands—
lifted first by friends probably gone,

Molly whined, on goofballs—
then those of strangers,
a danger so many-handed that it was divided

into affection as the body
jerked & was tossed toward the arena stage
spotlit for the heavy-metal band

self-proclaimed the Mammon of Iniquity,
who had brushed themselves red,
their dog-collared vocalist,
to himself or to the thousands, acting out

a sexual riff on love.

Those Condemned by Appetite
to Eat Themselves

> He must go by another way who would escape
> this wilderness...
>
> DANTE: *The Inferno*

Two weeks into the night shifts,
I patched together sleep
until Saturdays started near noon,

when holes in the shade spurted
sun. Nights, the two-transfer rides
to the factory, I dozed,

nineteen, on my own, nearly feral,
doped on refrigerator scraps & rancor,
smelling the tomatoes that suppurated

through my lunch sack, my hands already
curling for the machine levers I hated.
I tried folding a *Trib* between

myself & the four other riders,
rode the news past a half hour of neons
until the dark glass showed

I should transfer—the factory district
where one night a razor cut
Xs in my shirt, where in another test

I outran death, ironically hobbled
by the bus money I'd hidden
in one sock. All ride long I'd work out

the conspiracy of drivers & predators
until I knew seven dollars
was the least tribute I could lose

& had it ready so I wouldn't be cut deeper.
The August night I slept
a different route through Chicago's

three-street Italy, I woke to small fists
rat-a-tatting what I took
as one test more & next, through our bus metal,

a belligerent thunder as the opened
hydrant wet me down the window cracks
to my shoulder. I was burning

away in self-hate as I pressed myself
to the glass through which I saw children
pounding one another to get at a fallen man—

water that made them sensualists
wet equally the one clothed leg I saw
& their thin seminaked bodies

silvered ectoplasmic by the few streetlamps.
& in the hydrant's spray itself,
their little faces flicked parti-colored

as frog skin—one girl's nose over some wet
body part angled like an arm
in the polymorphous twining—feet so handlike

& hands so twiggy that I too twisted
briefly to their mocking of the test
they implied before the driver, my Virgil,

swerved us on to the next place—
where I too would be robbed.

Temporal Aspects of Dying as a Nonscheduled Status Passage

after the title of a sociology article

The backup in the nose is fruity
mouthwash; the nurse next swabs Xs
over his body holes—the arrows she draws

to them itch: man's years
are short, but his days are long.
In the sociology report, his name may be N —

X or Y in the lab notices.
His body's muddy yellow as he becomes
more obvious in the white-on-white

hospital thaw. But because researchers say
the dying redo to completion
one past symbolic act, in his head

he's snowshoeing the Donner Pass
of twenty years before,
old US 40 two meters down in grainy snow

according to the marker stakes
somebody's swabbed orange,
the slopes prickled with conifer

tips, the trees themselves
under downwind drifts
pocked by sun & torn across by slides.

Not twenty years ago, but now as doctors watch
he warms himself in the brief
chrome flash of cars from the new road

miles above him, a west sun forged
from a thousand thousand windshields:
resort skiers intent on home.

All day he has zigzagged the slope down
to the crevasse, a ten-foot-wide passage,
the snow at the edge, now as he touches

it barehanded, like cold suede.
He gives up snowshoes & bellyrides the crevasse
wall to the stream below, the blued snow

overhead & in the crevasse walls blued.
The stream takes the color
of whatever he could put into it.

He's sweating & his mouth tastes bad.
His thighs ache as he squats, not yet drinking.
His own blurred fingers color the snowmelt

now, *lacrimae rerum,* the liquid
so cold & his fingers
in it amplified, honest.

The Frog

Better my grandson's crayoned Easter pasteup,
his mâché Jesus ascendant,
pasty arms embracing raw blue

&, I think, better the cookie cutter animal,
this project the boy talks & talks about,
its unset dough skinned over,
& its jungle dyed with a pastry brush—

better all these than the real frog
the boy now shows me,
bobbling it down the hot August blocks

to me in his shirt front,
a suety nerve system,
composite of boy & cold prescience.
It hops on fine twigged feet,

not animal enough
even though the whole of it throbs
with heartbeats:
it's the heartbeats that turn

me sick with enticement,
the skin movements
around the eyes that are bubbled out

like a spearfishing Barbados diver's,
the eyes expanding as the body
under pressure goes dense
inside all that loose skin.

Now I don't want any more;
now I'm replete & less patient
as the boy explains the jungle

until I have it by heart—
as I had the Easter Lord
pasted over the other dead & brushed gold.
All the while the boy talks

I'm in the creek bottom between
stones, between soda cans crushed silvery.
As he talks, I'm in the vegetal
nullity the tadpoles come from, spinning

up in volleys toward the watery
sun of first hatch.

The Gregor Samsa Syndrome

My Nixon began when I did,
1960, the same summer marriage healed me.
Nixon's two-car caravan, lost between Convention

Hall & his Chicago hotel,
but only my arm's length away & two changes
from president—Kafka would've made him

smaller but Nixon's limo metal refracted
him big—light sliding,
unable to hold on to the dark metal as his limo

cornered. I had to stoop to see in
past my window reflection doubled
over his face, surprised by the Nixon nose

behind my own, the omnivorous
whisker shadow that only tired when it reached

his eyes or the jowls knotted
off with a rep tie—not yet Nixon enough.
Not insect, peripheral to the analogy
but infected by it, I was a Stockyards
guard—I indicated to him the straps

that crossed my heart;
with the other hand I remember I showed

the way out of the Stockyards.
Behind me, the closed packing plant gate,

so often spliced that it seemed to climb
itself wire by wire
into the twilight hazed like hairspray
above the soft, smog-bitten brick,

the zone of boarded factories—
Upton Sinclair's Chicago, relic & by then rat Gehenna.
I pointed north where several Chicagos
overlapped between Nixon's nomination

& his downtown hotel.
The lost campaign guide car, a fender ahead, crunched
over bottle fragments
as Nixon left me, a skinny summer hire

in twill some earlier fat guard
had sweated piebald—my uniform collar
furred with abrasions
& so capacious that I could tuck my chin

in under the tie. Economics had moved
the slaughter closer to the animal-breeding Iowa
& Kansas farms, moved it so far

west that just years later it showed up
human in Da Nang & Hue.
The old meatpacking kill rooms had no power,
though leftover electricity

still coated chutes, metal stairs & hatchways—
that whole summer I went
flashlit & scared, realizing that I was the only meat

in the half-dismantled plant & that the roaches
knew it. Handsful skittered
over one another when I popped

a switch the dismantlers had left in, & the bulb
might flash once, an aspirin
clouded by its own dissolve.
Sometimes that summer I'd be so lost

in those ghost wars,
the images of fat-knotted offal
steaming inside vats, the saved organs
still working the next world's foods, that

I'd have to trot my rounds by flashlight
&, almost too late, fumble
my alarm key into the company sequence,
the next box & the next box,
my flashlight skimming blood spots

in odd places: on a ceiling,
up one window grimed shut but poked
through the reinforcing mesh with ragged breath holes.
I'd stumble, lost—no machines left

but bolt holes in the floor, shafts open
under sawhorses. I'd stumble like a Stavrogin
arguing the missing steps to suicide—

the way my Nixon later died,
guilty of forgiving himself, a kind

of suicide. Forgive me if I only pointed him
away from my war. Now I'm over sixty,
chitinous & inarticulate but never Nixon's Virgil—
see, I'm not a Kafka, at most I'm an exegete

of Keats-scraplets, little milagros, anthology lines
I once copied to quote myself

into my wife's love.

About the Author

Dennis Schmitz was raised in Iowa and earned degrees at Loras College and the University of Chicago. He is the author of six books of poetry, including *About Night: Selected and New Poems* (Field). He has received numerous awards for his work, including the Shelley Memorial Award, two Pushcart Prizes, and fellowships from the Guggenheim Foundation and the National Endowment for the Arts. He taught for more than thirty years at California State University at Sacramento and served as a Poet Laureate of Sacramento.

The Chinese character for poetry is made up of two parts: "word" and "temple." It also serves as pressmark for Copper Canyon Press.

Founded in 1972, Copper Canyon Press remains dedicated to publishing poetry exclusively, from Nobel laureates to new and emerging authors. The Press thrives with the generous patronage of readers, writers, booksellers, librarians, teachers, students, and funders—everyone who shares the conviction that poetry invigorates the language and sharpens our appreciation of the world.

PUBLISHERS' CIRCLE
The Allen Foundation for the Arts
Lannan Foundation
National Endowment for the Arts

EDITORS' CIRCLE
Thatcher Bailey
The Breneman Jaech Foundation
Cynthia Hartwig and Tom Booster
Port Townsend Paper Company
Target Stores
Emily Warn and Daj Oberg
Washington State Arts Commission

For information and catalogs:

COPPER CANYON PRESS
Post Office Box 271
Port Townsend, Washington 98368
360/385-4925
www.coppercanyonpress.org

Set in Mrs. Eaves, Zuzana Licko's contemporary revival
of the Neoclassical typefaces of John Baskerville.

Book design and composition by
Valerie Brewster, Scribe Typography.
Printed on archival-quality Glatfelter Author's Text
at McNaughton & Gunn.

●◆●